NATIONAL GEOGRAPHIC

T0288453

Imagining the FUTURE

PIONEER EDITION

By Terri L. Jones and Susan Blackaby

CONTENTS

Thinking Tall. *In this painting, the artist imagines a city in the future. It has tall buildings and skyways.*

Back to the FUTURE

BY TERRI L. JONES

Does your family have a robot? Does your mom fly to work with a jetpack? In the 1950s, some people thought life would be like this in the twenty-first century. After all, anything is possible in the future.

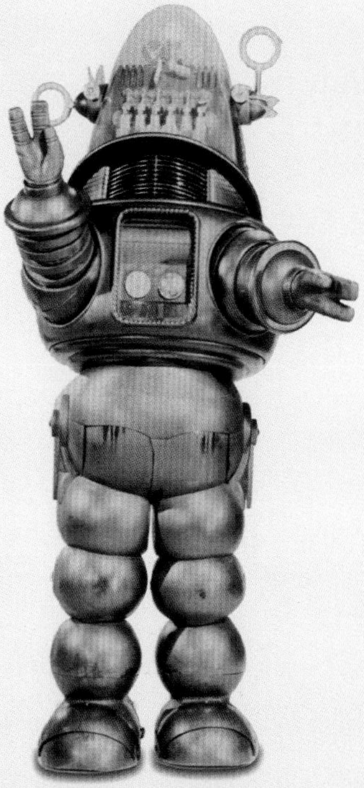

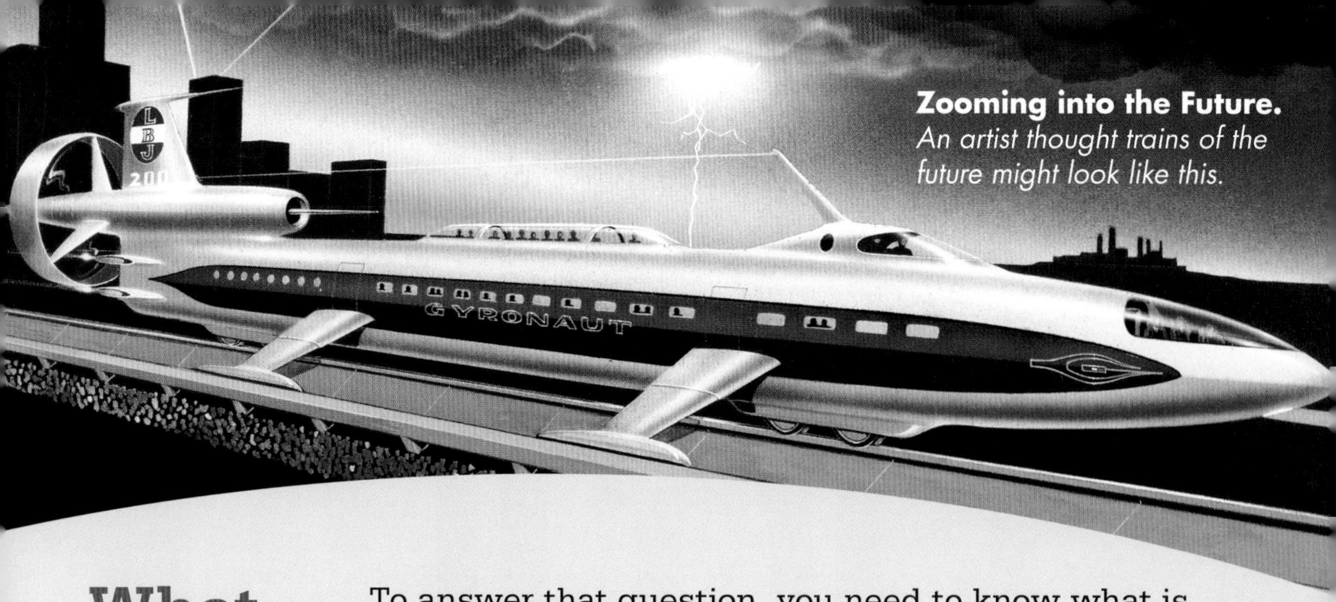

Zooming into the Future. *An artist thought trains of the future might look like this.*

What will the future bring?

To answer that question, you need to know what is possible. You also need imagination.

Science fiction stories can help give you ideas. Science fiction mixes real science with make-believe. Writers and engineers in the past imagined what life would be like the **twenty-first century**. Does your life look like what they predicted?

Home, Sweet Robot

In the 1950s, a science fiction book described an amazing house. It was a house of the future. Robots did all the chores. They cooked and cleaned. They set the table and vacuumed.

Today, robots really are on the job. They vacuum floors, cook meals, and build cars. Robots are even exploring outer space.

Disneyland had a "smart" house, too. The house almost ran itself. Today, many homes are run by automatic controls. Microwave ovens can cook meals in just minutes.

Cities in Space

Some **predictions** from the past were out of this world. How does a city in space sound? Some people thought we would live on the moon by the 1990s!

How would this work? Well, people would use hydroponics to grow their food. That means the plants would grow without soil. Energy from the sun would supply power.

Today, astronauts do live in a space station. They stay only a few months at a time, though. Some farms do grow plants without soil. Many homes on Earth use power from the sun. But a city in space is still many years away.

Present + Possible = Future

People also tried to think of new ways for people to communicate with each other in the future.

People already had telephones and TVs in the 1950s. The creators of a popular comic book and TV show put the two together!

The comic and TV show were about Dick Tracy. He was a smart and tough detective. He used his watch as a phone. The watch also let him see people while he talked to them. In real life, no one had a watch like Tracy's.

Today, many people watch videos on their cell phones. People use webcams to see each other on the Internet. What was only in stories in the 1950s is really possible today!

Moon City. *This artist thought of a city on the moon. Can you see the "Earthrise"?*

Take Off. *People once thought that in the future jetpacks would be used for everyday travel.*

Up, Up, But Not Away

Some people don't just imagine the future. They try to build it. Take the jetpack. This is a backpack with a small rocket engine. You put the pack on and start it up. Then you take off!

The jetpack isn't as great as it seems. It can't carry very much fuel, so it can't go very far. Also, the fuel is dangerous because it gets very, very hot! And the pack's loud engine can hurt your ears.

Still, a jetpack is a fun idea. Maybe one day someone will make the pack work. Until that time, you better count on the bus.

Getting From Here to There

Another cool idea was the flying car. It had wings. The car really worked! Flying cars didn't completely catch on. Maybe they were hard to park.

In one science fiction story, people jumped on moving belts to get around. That wasn't such a crazy idea. Today "people movers" carry travelers through airports. Escalators carry people up and down. There are even moving sidewalks in some places.

People in the 1950s dreamed of a car that drove itself. Today, that car is still a dream. But in time, that dream may come true, too.

Super Big Computer. *In the 1950s, computers were huge! Just one filled up a whole room.*

Fast Forward

In 1950, the only computers were very big. Each one filled a whole room! No one could imagine a personal computer. Then someone invented the computer chip. The tiny chip let engineers build small computers. Now, millions of people have their own computer at home.

The future of the 1950s is here. Think about your future. Will you fly to work with a jetpack? Will you live in an underwater city? Think big. Think fantastic! The future is yours to invent.

Wordwise

prediction: statement about what someone thinks might happen in the future

science fiction: storytelling that combines science with made-up events

twenty-first century: between 2001–2100 C.E.

PEDAL POWER

By Susan Blackaby

What is the quickest, easiest, coolest way to get from one place to another? One billion bike riders think they have the answer.

Bicycle riders are on the go. They pedal to work and to school. They ride for fun. Bikes are cheap and easy to use. You can learn to ride one in a week or so. But learning how to build today's modern bikes took many years.

Bumpy Beginnings

In the early 1800s, bikes were called "hobbyhorses." They didn't have pedals. Riders pushed their feet along the ground to move forward. It was not much better than walking!

Around 1860, bikes had pedals. That made the ride faster and more fun. These bikes were called "boneshakers" because they bumped and bounced along.

Then came the "high-wheeler." It had a huge front wheel—about 1.5 meters (5 feet) tall—and a tiny back wheel. Its wheels had metal spokes. They absorbed jolts on bumpy roads.

The rider sat up high and had to steer carefully. If the front wheel hit something, the rider could hit the ground headfirst!

Safe Arrival

Soon, bike makers added chains and gears to bikes. Gears let riders change speed and pedal less. Bike makers also made the wheels the same size. They added rubber tires, too. With these important **innovations**, the modern bicycle was born.

Making Progress

By the 1890s, bike riding was popular. Bumpy roads were paved over. This allowed bikes to travel more smoothly.

Bikes also inspired some important inventions. The Wright brothers used bike parts to invent their first flying machine in 1903. Henry Ford used bike parts to make his first car. These two inventions changed the world.

Pedal Pushing. *Hobbyhorses (near right) had no pedals. Riders pushed their feet on the ground. Boneshakers (far right) were the first bikes with pedals.*

Cruisers and Classics

Then cars were invented. Adults switched from pedaling to driving. So bike builders made bikes just for kids.

In the 1930s, bikes called Cruisers had balloon tires. Their wide rubber tires rolled right over bumps. Bikes called Classics had chrome fenders. Some had lights, bells, and streamers. Classics were sturdy and heavy.

Stunts and Speed

In the 1960s, California kids started a **trend**. They fit V-shaped handlebars on their bikes. The idea was used to build bikes that are good for stunts and riding on dirt. They were the first bikes used in BMX racing.

In the 1970s, gas prices went up, and air pollution was a problem. So adults got back on bikes. They liked ten-speed bikes. Extra gears made it easier to pedal uphill. Today, people ride these bikes in a famous race called the Tour de France.

To the Hills and Beyond

By the 1980s, some riders headed for the hills. They rode the first mountain bikes. These bikes were made from old Classics and Cruisers. Some mountain bikers do dangerous things. They go for teeth-jarring rides. They speed over sharp rocks and ragged roots. Their bikes really take a beating.

Other mountain bikers like to explore canyons and peaks. Their bikes need strong frames. They need to go up and down hills easily.

Today, there are many kinds of bikes: mountain bikes, racers, and BMX bikes. Fold-up bikes slide under a desk. Electronic bikes have their own power. There is even a bike you ride sideways, like a snowboard!

Now it's your turn. What new kind of bike could *you* design? What cool ideas to you have for bikes of the future? Start thinking! Then enjoy the ride!

Bikes
ACROSS TIME

Hobbyhorse
Early 1800s

Boneshaker
1860s

High-wheeler
1870s

Bikes and Balance. *To ride a high-wheeler bike, the rider sat on a seat high above the ground.*

Modern Racers. *Today's bikes let riders go faster than ever!*

WORD WISE

innovation: a new thing, idea, or way of doing something

trend: something that becomes very popular

Cruiser
1930s

High-rise
1960s

Mountain Bike
Late 1990s

Hi-Tech Bike
2012

THE FUTURE IS NOW

Look ahead to the future. Then answer these questions.

1. What did people from the 1950s predict about life in the future?
2. What twenty-first century invention did people from the 1950s not imagine?
3. Why did bike makers create Cruisers and Classic bicycles?
4. How are bicycles today like the first bikes? How are they different?
5. How is information organized in "Present + Possible = Future" and in "Bikes Across Time"?

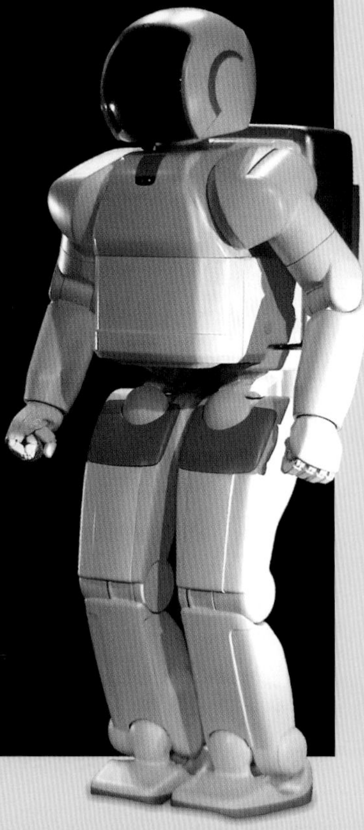